Smackers®
We Are Girls

by Suzanne

Scholastic Inc.

New York   Toronto   London   Auckland   Sydney

Mexico City   New Delhi   Hong Kong

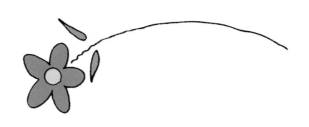

No part of this publication may be reproduced in whole or in part,
or stored in a retrieval system, or transmitted in any form or by any means,
electronic, mechanical, photocopying, recording, or otherwise,
without written permission of the publisher.

For information regarding permission, write to:
Scholastic Inc., Attention: Permissions Dept., 555 Broadway, New York, NY 10012.

ISBN 0-439-05847-3

Bonne Bell, Smackers, Lip Smacker, We Are Girls, Smackersville characters,
and associated logos are trademarks or registered trademarks of Bonne Bell, Inc.
All illustration and design content copyrighted by Bonne Bell, Inc.
© Bonne Bell, Inc. 2000

All rights reserved. Published by Scholastic Inc.

SCHOLASTIC and associated logos
are trademarks and/or registered trademarks of Scholastic, Inc.

12 11 10 9 8 7 6 5 4 3 2 1   0 1 2 3 4 5/0

Printed in the U.S.A   23

First Scholastic printing,
August 2000.

This book belongs to:

_____

_____

Contents

Just Me!

Best Friends!

My Style!

How to Use This Book

This book is just for girls like you! It's full of fantastic questions and funny quizzes that will tell you all you need to know about who you really are. It will make you laugh — and it will make you think.

You might want to keep your answers all to yourself. But you might also want to share this book with your best friend, just like you would your favorite magazine, since it contains lots of things for you to do together.

There's plenty of space in this book for you to decorate to make it your own! And be sure to come back to it weeks, even months, later to remember what was on your mind the last time you read it and answered the questions.

With **We Are Girls**, you'll have fun exploring absolutely everything about one awesome and amazing person — you!

Introduction

We've always known that it's great to be a girl.

When Jesse Bell started the Bonne Bell cosmetics company in 1927, he named it after his daughter Bonne. Since then, Bonne Bell has been geared toward girls just like you.

Bonne Bell became famous when it started making Lip Smackers, in 1973. The first Lip Smacker was Strawberry. Now there are over 60 flavors to collect, and you can find Smackers in over 20 countries around the world!

We are very much a family business. Now Jesse Bell's grandchildren are all grown up and our family includes his fourteen great-grandchildren! There are lots of boys in the family, but it's the girls who help us keep in touch with our customers.

Our girls do everything that you do. They're active, social, and busy. They enjoy having lots of friends — and lots of fun. They like this book, and we think you will, too.

This book is all about being a strong, happy, healthy girl. And so is Bonne Bell. Our motto is **"We Are Girls."** It means that we care about everything you care about. Bonne Bell has been here for girls like you for over seventy years. And with you in our extended family, we plan to be around for a whole lot longer!

Hilary Buddy

Hilary and Buddy Bell

Paste or draw a picture of yourself here

This is me on this date:

_____ / _____ / _____ / _____
day   month   date   year

Introducing Me!

My real, official name is:

_____ _____ _____
first   middle   last

Some people call me:_____

It would be cool
if my nickname were:_____

If I were a rock star
I'd call myself:_____

My hair is this color:_____

and is this long:_____

My eyes are:_____

I am:_____feet_____inches tall

I am:_____years old

My birthday is:_____ / _____ / _____
                         month   day   year

My birthstone is:_____

My astrological sign is:_____

_____

My lucky number is:_____

I'd use these words to describe myself:_____

_____   _____

_____   _____

_____   _____

_____   _____

This is the best thing about me:_____

_____

_____

_____

Here's a description of where I live:_____

_____

_____

_____

_____

_____

I have lived here since:_____

_____

Before that, I lived here:_____

_____

_____

These are the good things about where I live:_____

_____

_____

These things could be better, though:_____

_____

_____

_____

3

Each birthstone has a special quality!

Boysenberry Ruby

January's birthstone is a **GARNET** ...it gives you energy.

February's birthstone is an **AMETHYST**...it offers you peace and protection.

March's birthstone is an AQUAMARINE ...it keeps you calm.

April's birthstone is a **DIAMOND**...it guarantees that you will find true love.

May's birthstone is an EMERALD...it helps you to see the future.

June's birthstone is a PEARL...it keeps you healthy.

July's birthstone is a **RUBY**...it warns you if you're in danger.

August's birthstone is a PERIDOT ...it brings you happiness.

September's birthstone is a **SAPPHIRE** ...it keeps you honest.

October's birthstone is an OPAL...makes all your wishes come true.

November's birthstone is a TOPAZ...it increases your knowledge.

December's birthstone is TURQUOISE...it always brings you good luck.

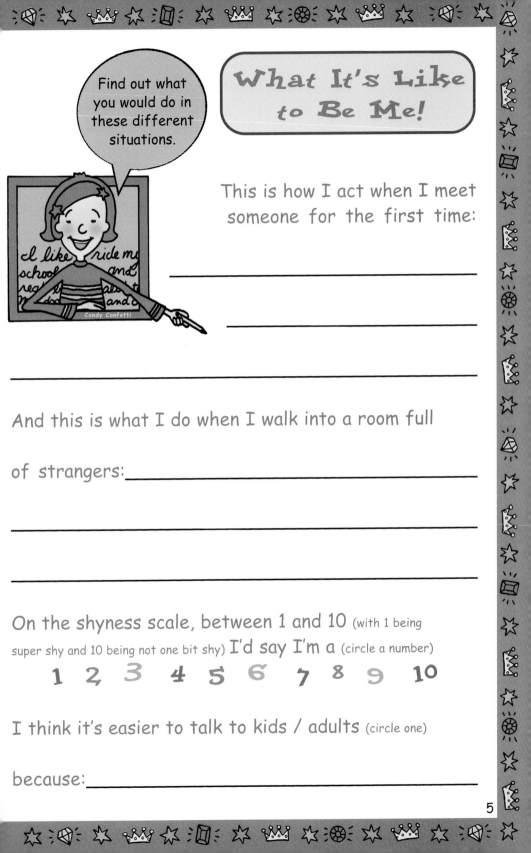

Find out what you would do in these different situations.

What It's Like to Be Me!

This is how I act when I meet someone for the first time:

_____

_____

_____

And this is what I do when I walk into a room full

of strangers:_____

_____

_____

On the shyness scale, between 1 and 10 (with 1 being super shy and 10 being not one bit shy) I'd say I'm a (circle a number)

1   2   3   4   5   6   7   8   9   10

I think it's easier to talk to kids / adults (circle one)

because:_____

_____

_____

I think it's easier to hang out with boys/girls (circle one)

because:_____

_____

_____

Here's how I feel when I'm away from home for more

than one night:_____

_____

_____

If I had to go to a new school, I'd probably act like this

on the first day:_____

_____

_____

_____

The last time I tried something new (a sport, a food, a new

hairstyle) was:_____

_____

_____

_____

I did / didn't (circle one) like it because:_____

_____

_____

Draw or paste in what it's like to be you

These are things I've heard other people say to

describe me:_____

_____

_____

I think they are / aren't (circle one) true because:_____

_____

_____

This is one thing I'd like to change about the way

I act:_____

_____

_____

But this is something I would never, ever change about

myself:_____

_____

_____

8

My Personality!
A Quiz

Uncover the true you when you take this quiz!

Bubblegum

The things we say and do reveal a lot about us.

Circle the answers that fit you best, then skip to the end to find out what they mean.

1. When is the best time for you to tackle a school report?

   a. in the morning.
   b. right after school.
   c. late at night.

2. When something strikes you as funny, what do you do?

   a. laugh so hard your sides hurt
   b. smile
   c. chuckle quietly

3. When talking on the phone, which of these do you do?

    a. walk all over the house
    b. sit back and relax
    c. try to do a million things at the same time

4. How do you usually sit?

    a. leaning to one side with your legs crossed
    b. cross-legged
    c. with your legs neatly side by side

5. If you're given something to eat that you don't like, you...

    a. say you don't like it, and ask for something else
    b. force it down anyway
    c. eat around it and leave what you don't like on the plate

6. When you talk to someone, which do you do?

    a. touch the other person on the arm or elbow
    b. fold your arms
    c. play with your hair

What Your Answers Say...

1. a. **in the morning.** You'll never need a cup of coffee to get you out of bed! You can't relax 'til something's finished — so you like to get started right away. Like most morning people, you're super-organized and super-motivated.

   b. **right after school.** You know you need to keep going while your energy is still high. Once you stop, you can't get started again. You'd rather goof off, but you know that what has to be done better be done right away — or it won't get done at all.

   c. **late at night.** You can only work when you're ready — even if it's after dark. Everything you do is inspired and creative — but you need to be sure you get enough sleep!

2. a. **laugh so hard your sides hurt.** You are outgoing and sure of yourself. You love a good time!

   b. **smile.** You don't like to draw attention to yourself. But you have a lot to offer — when you're ready to speak up.

   c. **chuckle quietly.** You try not to care much about what other people think.

3. a. **walk all over the house.** You think best when you're moving.

   b. **sit back and relax.** You're a good listener.

   c. **try to do a million other things at the same time.** Your boundless energy can make you a good leader. But sometimes you get carried away by taking on too much.

4. a. **leaning to one side with your legs crossed.** This position shows you're interested in what people have to say, and it makes them feel they have your attention. You're leaning in to hear their words — but your crossed legs signal that you won't speak until you've heard the whole story.
   b. **cross-legged.** You're casual and easygoing. You've never had any trouble opening up to people.
   c. **with your legs neatly side by side.** Some say this position shows good manners! It shows that you're listening to the other person even if you don't agree with what he or she is saying.

5. a. **say you don't like it and ask for something else.** You're bold and outspoken — you see no point in hiding the truth. You don't always think before you speak, but you do try to be aware of others' feelings.
   b. **force it down anyway.** You go to great lengths to be kind, but sometimes you forget to be kind to yourself!
   c. **eat around it and leave what you don't like on the plate.** You're aware of both your needs and the needs of those around you — that's why you're able to get along with anybody.

6. a. **touch the other person on the arm or elbow.** You want to draw people into your world.
   b. **fold your arms.** You wait until you really know a person before opening up. Until then, you keep people at a distance.
   c. **play with your hair.** You're fun-loving and playful. Playing with your hair may indicate that you're listening to the other person and thinking about what you're going to say next. But some people may think that your hair is distracting you from what they have to say!

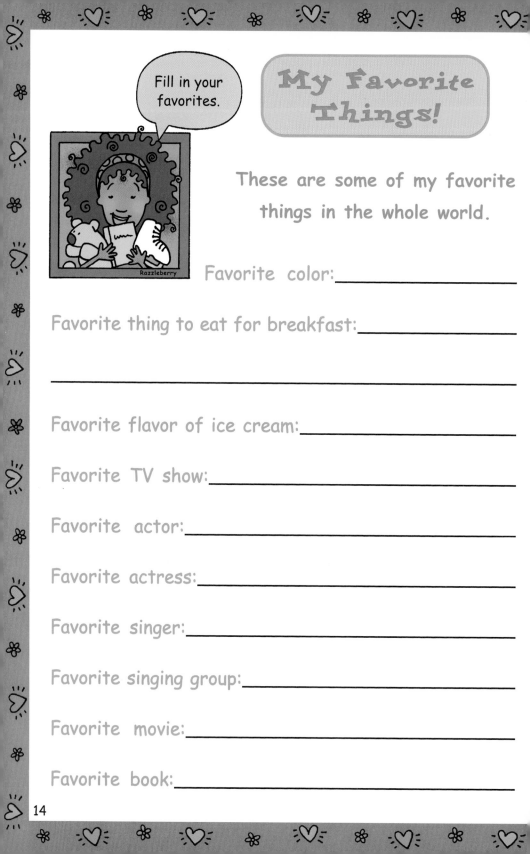

Fill in your favorites.

My Favorite Things!

These are some of my favorite things in the whole world.

Favorite color:_____

Favorite thing to eat for breakfast:_____

_____

Favorite flavor of ice cream:_____

Favorite TV show:_____

Favorite actor:_____

Favorite actress:_____

Favorite singer:_____

Favorite singing group:_____

Favorite movie:_____

Favorite book:_____

Draw or paste in some of your

favorite things here.

Favorite season:_____

Favorite place to be in a snowstorm:_____

_____

Favorite person to walk in the rain with:_____

_____

Favorite birthday gift of all time:_____

_____

Favorite thing to do on Saturday morning:_____

_____

_____

Favorite thing to do at recess:_____

_____

Favorite thing to do on summer vacation:_____

_____

_____

Favorite place to shop with friends:_____

_____

Favorite outfit:_____

Favorite way to put off homework:_____

_____

Favorite musical instrument:_____

Favorite board game:_____

Favorite video game:_____

Favorite thing to do with my siblings:_____

_____

_____

Favorite way to show my parents I love them:_____

_____

_____

Favorite Lip Smacker:_____

This quiz will tell you things you never knew about yourself!

Razzleberry

Figuring Out My Favorites

Answer each question by choosing what you like best.

At the end of this section, you'll find out what your choices say about you.

1. Pick a favorite from these five:
   a. cocker spaniel
   b. racehorse
   c. robin
   d. butterfly
   e. penguin

2. Which of these colors do you like best?:
   a. pink
   b. green
   c. blue
   d. red
   e. purple

3. Which of these styles of music do you like best?
   a. pop
   b. alternative
   c. country
   d. classical
   e. rock

4. Which of these types of movies do you like best?
   a. serious drama
   b. comedy
   c. horror
   d. real-life drama
   e. science fiction

5. Which of these jewels do you like most?

   a. diamond
   b. ruby
   c. emerald
   d. sapphire
   e. pearl

6. Which of these would you choose to study?

   a. ancient Egypt
   b. mythology
   c. cooking
   d. rocket science
   e. psychology

7. Which of these shapes is your favorite?

   a. heart
   b. circle
   c. star
   d. hexagon
   e. square

8. Where would you most like to be right now?

   a. the country
   b. the city
   c. the suburbs
   d. the mountains
   e. the beach

What Your Answers Mean

1. a. **cocker spaniel.** You always try to be helpful. Even when it's hard, you're loyal to your friends.
   b. **racehorse.** You're strong in both body and spirit.
   c. **robin.** Above all, you encourage your friends to be themselves.
   d. **butterfly.** You're carefree, and you like to go where your moods take you.
   e. **penguin.** You have a great sense of humor. You appreciate people for who they are — it doesn't matter to you if they're popular.

19

2. a. **pink.** You're confident and outgoing.
    b. **green.** Your energy lights up wherever you are.
    c. **blue.** You are sometimes quiet, but friends seek you out because you're peaceful and calm.
    d. **red.** You're bold and beautiful, and nothing gets in your way.
    e. **purple.** You can easily get lost in your own thoughts.

3. a. **pop.** You're upbeat and on top of the latest trends.
    b. **alternative.** You throw yourself passionately into lots of causes.
    c. **country.** You cry at the drop of a hat!
    d. **classical.** You're truly independent. You like order and tradition.
    e. **rock.** You care deeply about other people.

4. a. **serious drama.** You're thoughtful and intelligent.
    b. **comedy.** You can see the funny side of any situation.
    c. **horror.** You're brave and you like to test the limits. You're drawn to any kind of excitement.
    d. **real-life drama.** You like to know about how real people deal with real situations. You'd rather not waste your time with things that aren't true.
    e. **science fiction.** To you, there's nothing more important than a good imagination!

5. a. **diamond**. You do everything with high style!
   b. **ruby**. You follow your heart, wherever it leads you.
   c. **emerald**. You feel you can get away with a lot — and most of the time you're right!
   d. **sapphire**. You often get your own way because you're both stubborn and charming.
   e. **pearl**. You like to daydream and take long walks.

6. a. **ancient Egypt**. You're willing to stretch your mind.
   b. **mythology**. You like to think about what brings people together, not what drives them apart.
   c. **cooking**. You enjoy working with your hands.
   d. **rocket science**. You don't give up easily — even when others do. You like the challenge of struggling to understand something really hard.
   e. **psychology**. You like to know why people do the things they do.

7. a. **heart**. You believe that anything is possible.
   b. **circle**. You hate to be left out of anything.
   c. **star**. You're not afraid to take the lead in doing what's right.
   d. **hexagon**. You like to have lots of choices and you're convinced that every problem has more than one solution.
   e. **square**. You're sensible, and you're always the first one to come through in an emergency.

8. a. **country.** You appreciate peace and quiet.
   b. **city.** You like to be on the go.
   c. **suburbs.** To you, the most imporant thing in the world is family.
   d. **mountains.** You love to tackle big challenges.
   e. **beach.** You are thoughtful and artistic.

There are all kinds of families.

Melon and Family

My Family!

Here's the 411 on my family.

These are the people in my

family:_____

_____

_____

_____

_____

These are the animals in my family:_____

_____

_____

_____

My grandparents are named:_____

_____

_____

_____

Here are some other relatives we see a lot:_____

_____

_____

_____

This is my favorite family tradition—I will hand it down

to my own family someday:_____

_____

_____

_____

_____

The most fun my family ever had together was:_____

_____

_____

_____

The best family holiday I can remember was:_____

_____

_____

_____

The best trip my family took together was:_____

_____

_____

_____

Here's something hilarious one of my relatives did (or said):

_____

_____

_____

But here's something really embarrassing somebody in

my family once did (or said):_____

_____

_____

Sometimes people in my family disagree about:_____

_____

_____

My brother/sister (circle one) drives me crazy when

he/she (circle one) :_____

_____

_____

_____

_____

_____

_____

This is what I like to do when I have my parents all to

myself:_____

_____

_____

_____

Here's what I love the best about my family:_____

_____

_____

_____

_____

_____

26

Birth Order

Where do you stand in your family? And what does it mean?

If you're the oldest, you're a natural leader.

If you're an only child, you're comfortable being by yourself.

If you're one of many, you're able to make yourself stand out.

If you're a twin, you never mind being asked to share.

If you're in the middle, you're good at ending any argument.

If you're the youngest, you're creative and likely to get your own way.

Draw or paste in some of your
favorite family memories here.

Write in some more things about yourself.

Only my family
and closest friends know
these things about me.

I'm thankful that I have these good qualities (be sure to fill in every blank!):

_____

_____

_____

_____

_____

This is something that makes me feel really, really

proud of myself:_____

_____

_____

_____

_____

_____

_____

Here's a celebrity I look up to:_____

_____

I think we have these things in common:_____

_____

_____

But I'd like to be more like him / her in these ways:____

_____

_____

Here's another person I look up to (someone I actually know):____

_____

_____

I think we have these things in common:_____

_____

_____

_____

But I'd like to be more like him / her in these ways:____

_____

_____

_____

_____

I'd say that this person is my role model._____

_____

because:_____

_____

_____

_____

To me, this is the very best thing about being

a girl:_____

_____

_____

_____

In fact, if I had to come up with a slogan for being

a girl, this is what it would be:_____

_____

Draw or paste in the very best thing
about being a girl.

Which flavor and scent do you like best?

Flavorful Me!

Nature is full
of amazing sights
and scents!

Which do you like best?
And what does it mean?
Choose the answers that fit you best,
then read on for an explanation!

1. **Which of these fruits tastes the best to you?**

   a. watermelon
   b. strawberry
   c. blueberry

2. **Which of these flower scents appeals to you most?**

   a. rose
   b. honeysuckle
   c. violet

3. **Which of these perfume names appeals to you?**

   a. Sweet Lavender
   b. Happy Hyacinth
   c. Forever Lily

4. For a boy or man, you think it's best if his cologne smells like:

   a. leather
   b. pine trees
   c. soap

5. Which of these air freshener sprays would you buy?

   a. vanilla
   b. strawberry-kiwi
   c. watermelon

What Your Answers Mean

1. a. **watermelon.** You like things that are truly unusual — someday you might travel to faraway places!
   b. **strawberry.** You like everything around you to be fresh and clean.
   c. **blueberry.** You like to remember good meals and good times.

2. a. **rose.** Your room should be airy with plenty of sunshine.
   b. **honeysuckle.** Your favorite season is summer, when you can talk and sip lemonade with your friends.
   c. **violet.** Curling up with a good mystery novel is your idea of fun.

3. a. **Sweet Lavender.** You are strong-willed and smart.
   b. **Happy Hyacinth.** You're a romantic type, full of daydreams and fantasies.
   c. **Forever Lily.** You love plants and animals — you're a nature girl!

4. a. **leather.** You like to know how things work.
   b. **pine trees.** You love to explore the outdoors.
   c. **soap.** You love when things in your life are neat and clean.

5. a. **vanilla.** You want your home to smell like fresh-baked cookies!
   b. **strawberry-kiwi.** If you could, you'd live in a tent in a beautiful field.
   c. **watermelon.** You're happiest at the seashore — you like big open spaces and the sound of the pounding surf.

It's important to have dreams.

My Hopes and Dreams!

Here is what might be in my future!

This is a career I think I might like when I grow up:_____

because:_____

_____

_____

But here's something I can't picture myself doing:_____

because:_____

_____

_____

I'd like to live here:_____

because:_____

_____

Here's how I think I might look:_____

_____

_____

_____

This is the kind of person I would like to marry:_____

_____

_____

_____

_____

If I have children, I'll probably have this many:_____

_____

And I really like all of these names:_____

_____

_____

_____

I'd like to have these pets:_____

_____

_____

Here are some friends I think I'll still keep in touch

with:_____

_____

_____

_____

These are some places I'd like to visit when I'm

grown up:_____

_____

_____

_____

_____

_____

This is something I'll be well known for:_____

_____

_____

_____

_____

_____

These are some great things I hope will never change

in my life:_____

_____

_____

_____

_____

_____

The Best of the Best!

My best friend
is the best ever!

Here's what you need
to know about my best
friend — and about a few
other people, too.

This person is my very best friend

in the whole world:_____

_____

Strawberry, Starfruit, and Melon

And here's why:_____

_____

_____

_____

The nicest thing my best friend ever did for me was:

_____

_____

_____

_____

Here's a funny thing that happened to us once:_____

_____

_____

_____

We got in trouble when we:_____

_____

_____

_____

I'd use these words to describe my best friend:_____

_____

_____

_____

And here's why I think we'll be best friends forever:

_____

_____

_____

I think of these people as good friends, too:_____

_____

_____

And I'd like to become better friends with:_____

_____

because:_____

_____

_____

These are my favorite things to do with my best

friend:_____

_____

_____

_____

Sometimes my BF bothers me when:_____

_____

_____

_____

Here's what I've said about it:_____

_____

_____

_____

The best part about being best friends is:_____

_____

_____

_____

_____

43

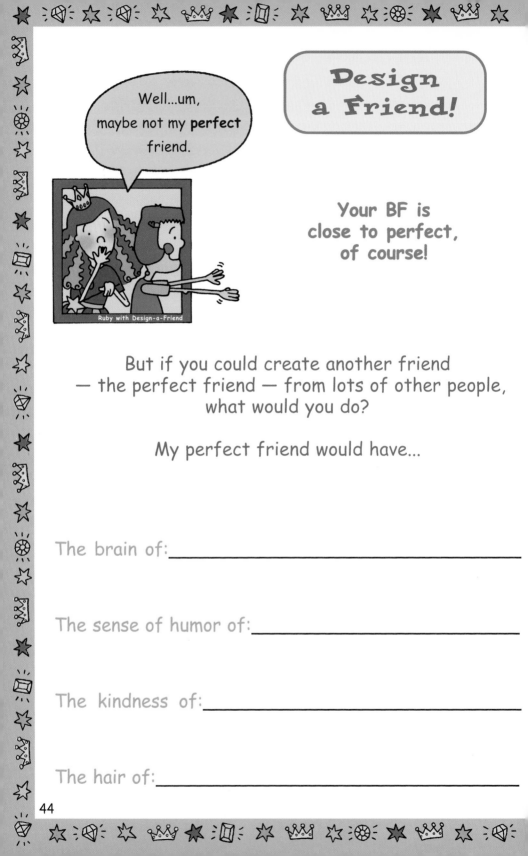

Well...um, maybe not my **perfect** friend.

Design a Friend!

Ruby with Design-a-Friend

Your BF is close to perfect, of course!

But if you could create another friend — the perfect friend — from lots of other people, what would you do?

My perfect friend would have...

The brain of:_____

The sense of humor of:_____

The kindness of:_____

The hair of:_____

The laugh of:_____

The athletic ability of:_____

The style of:_____

The singing voice of:_____

The dancing ability of:_____

The helpfulness of:_____

The listening ability of:_____

The good advice of:_____

The energy of:_____

The loyalty of:_____

Try writing your own advice column.

How do you handle problems with your friends?

Give your opinion to some people who are stuck in some tough situations.

Copycat Calamity

Help! I love my best friend, but she copies everything I do! If I get something new, she gets it, too. It's driving me nuts! But I don't know how to tell her without hurting her feelings. What should I do?

Here's what I'd say:_____

_____

_____

_____

_____

New-Friend Feud

I have just met a girl I like a lot. I'd like to spend more time getting to know her. But my best friend is sooo jealous! She's always making cracks about this new girl. She doesn't want her around. What should I do?

Here's what I'd say:_____

_____

_____

_____

_____

Cheating Best Friend

My best friend cheats on tests. Besides that, she's very funny and a great friend. But the cheating really bothers me. I want to stay friends, but I feel strange about the way she acts. I don't know what to do.

Here's what I'd say:_____

_____

_____

_____

_____

Moving Day Blues

I'm a wreck. My family has to move. My BF says she'll e-mail and call, but what if she doesn't? I can't stand the idea that our friendship might be over soon. I cry all the time. What can I do to feel better?

Here's what I'd say:_____

_____

_____

_____

_____

Here's a picture of my best friend and me!

Read Your Friend's Writing

What's the right way to read your friend's writing?

If she has big writing,
she has a big heart.

If she has small writing,
she's a little shy.

If she writes in a straight line,
she's a careful person.

If her writing slants across the page,
she has a good imagination.

If her dots are right over her i's,
she's hard-working.

If her dots are far away from her i's,
she's forgetful.

If she crosses her t's with a thick line,
she's a loud person.

If she crosses her t's with a thin line,
she's a quieter person.

If she always writes in script,
she's old-fashioned.

If she never writes in script,
she's always in touch with the trends.

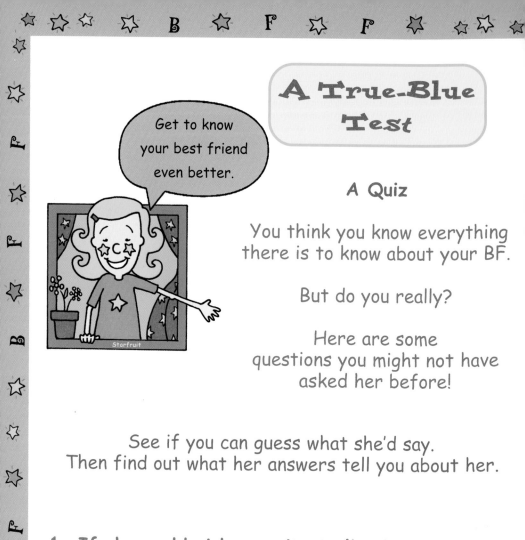

A True-Blue Test

Get to know your best friend even better.

Starfruit

A Quiz

You think you know everything there is to know about your BF.

But do you really?

Here are some questions you might not have asked her before!

See if you can guess what she'd say.
Then find out what her answers tell you about her.

1. **If she could pick one city to live in, it would be:**

   a. New York
   b. Paris
   c. Boston
   d. Rome

2. **Her favorite flower is:**

   a. rose
   b. lavender
   c. honeysuckle
   d. violet

3. Her personality is most like:

    a. fire
    b. water
    c. earth
    d. air

4. Her favorite type of dance is:

    a. ballet
    b. hip-hop
    c. square dance
    d. free style

5. Her favorite part of nature is:

    a. the afternoon sun
    b. the sky
    c. grass
    d. the rising sun

What the Answers Mean

1. a. New York. Your best friend is ambitious and talented — she'll work as hard as it takes to be a big success.
   b. Paris. She'll be setting new trends before long!
   c. Boston. She cares deeply about family and she's not afraid to speak her mind.
   d. Rome. She never takes anything at face value — instead, she looks beneath the surface.

2. a. **rose**. Your BF loves drama — maybe she should be onstage!
   b. **lavender**. She's the kind of person that everyone wants to be around.
   c. **honeysuckle**. She has no patience with people who are two-faced.
   d. **violet**. She always has a twinkle in her eye and a smile on her face.

3. a. **fire**. People think your best friend is strong and bold.
   b. **water**. People think she has an amazing imagination.
   c. **earth**. People trust her with even their deepest secrets.
   d. **air**. People always admire how smart she is.

4. a. **ballet**. To your BF, beauty is what matters most.
   b. **hip-hop**. She thinks strength matters most.
   c. **square dance**. She thinks people matter most.
   d. **free style**. She thinks freedom matters most.

5. a. **the afternoon sun**. Your BF always looks on the bright side of things.
   b. **the sky**. She's a quiet type, always looking for a peaceful place where she can think things through.
   c. **grass**. Her feelings are hurt easily.
   d. **the rising sun**. She has energy to spare!

Is your friendship for now or forever?

Bubblegum and Melon

Forever and Ever!

A Quiz

Will you really
be friends forever?

You can find out
for sure!

Just answer these questions honestly
and add up your points below.

1. Your report card arrived today — and it's
   much worse than you expected. You're really
   upset. You:

   a. call your best friend right away
   b. call someone who doesn't get such good grades
   c. keep it to yourself and hope your parents
      aren't too upset

2. Your friend suggests you buy matching outfits.
   You:

   a. think that's a great idea
   b. think "not again!" — she's always copying
   c. laugh and hope she's joking

3. If someone invited your pal to a party without you, she'd:

   a. accept — and ask if it was okay for you to come, too
   b. tell you all about it to show you how popular she is
   c. sneak off to the party without telling you

4. You and your BF agree on music, school, and sports:

   a. never
   b. sometimes
   c. usually

5. Here's how the two of you like to spend time together:

   a. alone, just the two of you
   b. with a bigger group of kids
   c. sometimes a and sometimes b

Add Up Your Score

Add up the numbers below, then read on to find out how your friendship scores.

1. a = 3   b = 2   c = 1
2. a = 3   b = 2   c = 1
3. a = 3   b = 2   c = 1
4. a = 1   b = 2   c = 3
5. a = 3   b = 1   c = 2

Friends Forever!   11 to 15 points

You two have so much in common! You see almost everything the same way. Your friendship has a good chance of lasting a lifetime, no matter where you move.

Best Buds!   6 to 10 points

You're not the same, but you have a lot to offer each other. Where she's weak, you're strong — and the other way around. You make a good team, but sometimes you clash. Sometimes it takes extra energy to stay in sync, but it's still worth the effort.

Fast Friends!   5 points

This friendship is a lot of fun right now, so enjoy it. But your answers show you might not be building something that will stand the test of time.

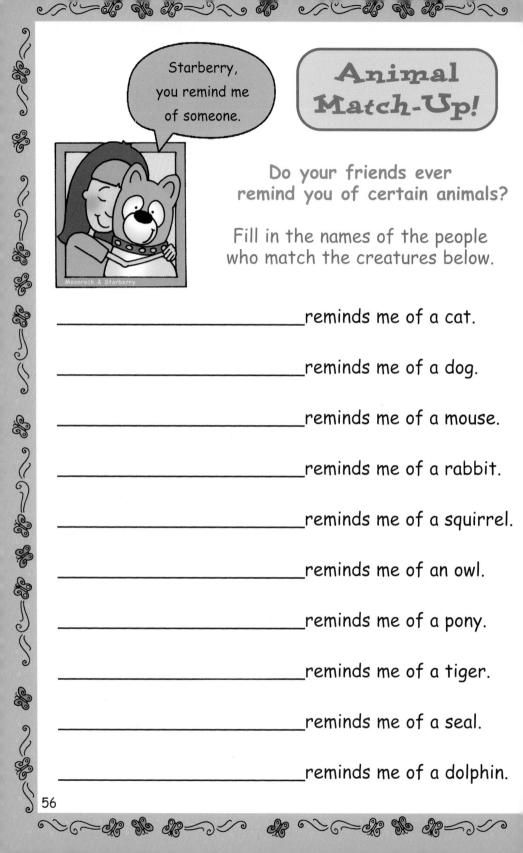

Starberry, you remind me of someone.

Animal Match-Up!

Do your friends ever remind you of certain animals?

Fill in the names of the people who match the creatures below.

_____reminds me of a cat.

_____reminds me of a dog.

_____reminds me of a mouse.

_____reminds me of a rabbit.

_____reminds me of a squirrel.

_____reminds me of an owl.

_____reminds me of a pony.

_____reminds me of a tiger.

_____reminds me of a seal.

_____reminds me of a dolphin.

The Best Friend Who's Always There

Take this quiz to find out if you are being your own best friend!

A Quiz

Guess who?
It's you!

It's important to be
a good friend to yourself.

But are you doing the best you can?
Take this quiz and find out.

1. If it was late, but your friend wanted you to stay on the phone listening to her problems, you'd:

    a. listen as long as you could but suggest you talk more tomorrow
    b. listen 'til you were so exhausted you couldn't get up the next day
    c. tell her you were tired and would rather talk later

2. When you fail at something you've tried, you:

    a. get so mad at yourself that you can't look in the mirror
    b. say, "Who cares?"
    c. figure out what you've learned — and how you can do better next time

57

3. When you want to do one thing,
   but your friend wants to do another,
   you:

   a. agree to do her thing — if she does what
      you want later
   b. tell her it's your way or no way
   c. do what she wants in case she gets mad

4. When you're alone, you:

   a. enjoy the time by yourself
   b. are totally bored
   c. call everyone you've ever met

5. If you had a new skirt your friend loved,
   you'd:

   a. give it to her.
   b. start saving to buy her one like it.
   c. encourage her to get the exact same one.

Add Up Your Score

Add up your answers to see where you stand.

1.	a = 5	b = 3	c = 1
2.	a = 3	b = 1	c = 5
3.	a = 5	b = 1	c = 3
4.	a = 5	b = 3	c = 1
5.	a = 3	b = 1	c = 5

Here's What Your Score Means

You're a Good Friend   17 to 25 points

You know how to be a good friend to others and still keep your own needs in mind.

Remember to Remember You   10 to 16 points

Remember that you deserve attention, too!

Your Own Best Friend   5 to 9 points

You put yourself first most of the time. You're so good to yourself that you might even have a hard time keeping friends.

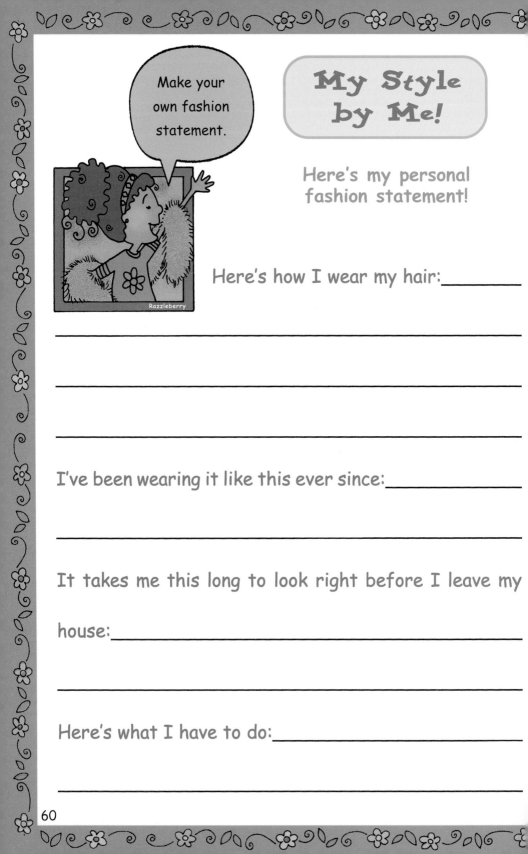

Make your own fashion statement.

My Style by Me!

Here's my personal fashion statement!

Razzleberry

Here's how I wear my hair:_____

_____

_____

_____

I've been wearing it like this ever since:_____

_____

It takes me this long to look right before I leave my

house:_____

_____

Here's what I have to do:_____

_____

_____

_____

_____

Here's where I like to get my hair cut:_____

_____

This is how often I cut it:_____

_____

I have (circle one) long nails / short nails.

When I paint them, my favorite color is:_____

_____

I think this is the best clothing in my closet:_____

_____

_____

_____

_____

If I could shop absolutely anywhere, it would be:_____

_____

_____

If I could get anything I wanted there, it would be:____

_____

_____

This is the kind of jewelry I like to wear:_____

_____

_____

My favorite piece of jewelry is my:_____

_____

_____

My favorite shoes are my:_____

_____

_____

I (circle one) do / don't like to wear dresses because:_____

_____

_____

_____

_____

Draw or paste in your personal style

What's my style?

Passionfruit

Finding Your Personal Style!

Are you totally stylin'?
Fabulously feminine?
Or bold and sporty?
Take this test to find out.

1. This is your idea of cool sneakers:

    a. platforms
    b. comfortable ones I can wear anywhere
       to do anything
    c. canvas ones with a flower design
       and colored laces

2. What color do you paint your nails for school?

    a. clear
    b. blue
    c. pink

3. At night you like to wear:

    a. cute pj's or a nightshirt with a colorful pattern
    b. a flowered or plaid nightgown
    c. sweats or a big T-shirt

4. Your favorite haircut is:

    a. the latest style
    b. long with an occasional trim
    c. as short as possible

5. This is your favorite sort of bag:
   a. a canvas backpack
   b. a crocheted bag
   c. a blue vinyl backpack

What Your Answers Mean

Each of your answers falls into
one of these categories:

TS - totally stylin'

FF - fabulously feminine

BNS - bold and sporty

Add Up Your Score

Once you figure out what
your answers are, you can find out what
your style tells the world!

1.	2.	3.	4.	5.
a. TS	a. BNS	a. TS	a. TS	a. BNS
b. BNS	b. TS	b. FF	b. FF	b. FF
c. FF	c. FF	c. BNS	c. BNS	c. TS

Here's What Your Score Means

Mostly TS

If you have mostly TS, style will always be important to you. Make sure you stay on top of the trends by reading magazines and scouring the stores. Someday you'll probably start some trends of your own!

Mostly FF

If you have mostly FF, you enjoy being a girl. And why shouldn't you? You don't buy into old-fashioned ideas about girls being weaker or in any way less than guys. You just don't want to look like one!

Mostly BNS

If you have mostly BNS, you are an active, no-nonsense person. Fashion isn't all that interesting to you. You care about how you look, but you'd rather not think too much about it. For you, the most important thing is to be ready to do anything at any time. You wouldn't want the wrong shoes to stop you from having an adventure!

Star Signs

Are you compatible?

See if the stars
say you've chosen
a good friend!

Aries gets along great with Gemini, Leo, Libra, Sagittarius

Taurus gets along great with Cancer, Virgo, Capricorn, Pisces

Gemini gets along great with Aries, Leo, Libra, Aquarius

Cancer gets along great with Taurus, Virgo, Scorpio, Pisces

Leo gets along great with Aries, Gemini, Libra, Sagittarius

Virgo gets along great with Taurus, Cancer, Scorpio, Capricorn

Libra gets along great with Gemini, Leo, Libra, Sagittarius

Scorpio gets along great with Cancer, Virgo, Capricorn, Pisces

Sagittarius gets along great with Aries, Leo, Libra, Aquarius

Capricorn gets along great with Taurus, Virgo, Scorpio, Pisces

Aquarius gets along great with Aries, Gemini, Libra, Sagittarius

Pisces gets along great with Taurus, Cancer, Scorpio, Capricorn

How well do you know your star sign?

Moonrock Candy with Starberry

Are You Like Your Sign?

Your horoscope is supposed to tell you a lot about your personality!

But does it really?

Find your sign in this list and check off all the traits you have. Then go to the end to find out how well you fit with your sign.

1. **If you were born in the sign of Aries, March 21 to April 19, are you:**

   1. brave?
   2. active?
   3. confident?
   4. determined?
   5. likely to believe every compliment?

2. **If you were born in the sign of Taurus, April 20 to May 20, are you:**

   1. careful?
   2. charming?
   3. patient?
   4. dependable?
   5. always honest?

3. If you were born in the sign of Gemini, May 21 to June 21, are you:

   1. moody?
   2. unpredictable?
   3. independent?
   4. athletic?
   5. unable to make up your mind?

4. If you were born in the sign of Cancer, June 22 to July 22, are you:

   1. home-loving?
   2. moody?
   3. creative?
   4. loyal?
   5. water-loving?

5. If you were born in the sign of Leo, July 23 to Aug. 22, are you:

   1. a leader?
   2. brave?
   3. worried about how you look?
   4. quick to make up your mind?
   5. energetic?

6. If you were born in the sign of Virgo, Aug. 23 to Sept. 22, are you:

   1. a leader?
   1. a quick thinker?
   2. creative?
   3. logical?
   4. able to make any situation work for you?
   5. able to fit in anywhere?

7. If you were born in the sign of Libra, Sept. 23 to Oct. 23, are you:

   1. fair?
   2. honest?
   3. easy to get along with?
   4. a little lazy?
   5. kind?

8. If you were born in the sign of Scorpio, Oct. 24 to Nov. 21, are you:

   1. energetic?
   2. jealous?
   3. ambitious?
   4. a dreamer?
   5. worried about how you look?

9. If you were born in the sign of Sagittarius, Nov. 22 to Dec. 21, are you:

   1. outgoing?
   2. honest?
   3. never two-faced?
   4. funny?
   5. sometimes forgetful of other's feelings?

10. If you were born in the sign of Capricorn, Dec. 22 to Jan. 19, are you:

   1. sensible?
   2. able to get things done quickly?
   3. gifted with a good memory?
   4. likely to hold a grudge?
   5. hardworking?

11. If you were born in the sign of Aquarius, Jan. 20 to Feb. 18, are you:

    1. a dreamer?
    2. reasonable?
    3. a fast learner?
    4. loyal?
    5. easily frustrated?

12. If you were born in the sign of Pisces, Feb. 19 to March 20, are you:

    1. creative?
    2. smart?
    3. imaginative?
    4. sometimes unable to act?
    5. optimistic?

The Results...

If you scored 4 or more yes answers, you're totally true to your sign.

But if you scored three, look to the sign directly before or after yours — you may have traits from that sign, too. This often happens to people born close to the days when the signs change.

If you have none or few of the traits listed for your sign, then maybe the horoscope just doesn't work for you. Keep in mind, though, that astrologers say your sign isn't all that matters in forming your personality — the alignment of the planets at your birth can also make its mark on who you are.

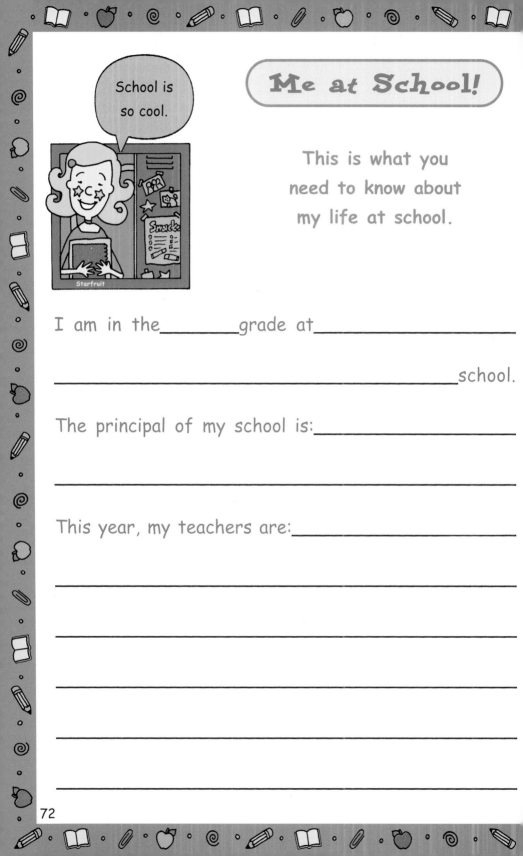

School is so cool.

Me at School!

This is what you need to know about my life at school.

Starfruit

I am in the_____grade at_____

_____school.

The principal of my school is:_____

_____

This year, my teachers are:_____

_____

_____

_____

_____

_____

The nicest teacher I ever had was:_____

_____

because:_____

_____

_____

The meanest teacher I ever had was:_____

_____

because:_____

_____

_____

The funniest teacher I ever had was:_____

_____

because:_____

_____

_____

The most unfair thing I ever saw a teacher do was:

_____

_____

_____

The kindest thing I ever saw a teacher do was:_____

_____

_____

_____

The school project I'm most proud of was:_____

_____

_____

_____

_____

Here are some of the awards I've won in school:_____

_____

But I was really embarrassed when this happened

to me in school:_____

_____

_____

Besides eating, this is what I like to do at lunchtime:

_____

_____

_____

This is my favorite game to play in gym:_____

_____because:_____

_____

_____

This is my very favorite thing to do after school:_____

_____

_____

_____

And my favorite subject in school is:_____

_____because:_____

_____

_____

_____

Draw or paste in your school style

I think math is my favorite subject.

Your Favorite Subject

Here's what it means if you like these subjects best!

Math — You enjoy order and logic.

Social Studies — Someday you will see the world!

Science — You believe in experimenting.

English — You feel that if you say something, you should say it well.

Art — You like things best when they're beautiful.

Gym — You like to move and you like to win!

Music — Rhythm and melody express your feelings better than words ever could.

Computer — You're a fast thinker.

Lunch — You might be a little bit too social!

Find out about your school style.

Candy Confetti

School Style!

**Where do you sit?
How do you answer?
Are you attentive?**

Look under each
question to learn about
your school style!

1. **When I can pick my seat, here's where I sit:**

   Your seating style says a lot about your confidence as a student.

a. If you head to the back it says, "Don't pick on me. Pretend I'm not here." Teachers think that unprepared students sit in the back. (Even though that's not always true.)

b. Sitting in the front, though, says you really want to participate. Teachers appreciate this and tend to pay more attention to kids who sit in the front. For those who can handle the spotlight (or want to impress the teacher) it's a great seat.

c. The middle is...well...the middle. Sitting there tells the teacher you're part of the group and listening but not ready to jump in with answers. Try moving one seat closer to the front every time you sit down.

2. When I know the answer to a question, I:

The way you answer says as much about you as where you sit.

a. Shooting your hand up shows that you've done the homework. Get right in there and go for it! Some students know the answer but think it's uncool to volunteer. This isn't a great strategy. If you've done your work, you should let it show. It's never uncool to be smart.

b. Then there are students who think they know the answer but aren't sure they're right. So, rather than embarrass themselves by giving a wrong answer, they decide to keep quiet. They don't realize it's better to take a chance. Teachers appreciate participation more than you can imagine. And being wrong is no biggie. It happens to everyone sometimes.

c. Finally, if you never answer because you never know the answer — get some extra help in the subject from your teacher, a parent, a tutor, or a friend.

3. When a teacher catches me daydreaming, I:

Do you pretend you were listening to the teacher? Do you turn red? Do you think fast and try to convince the teacher the plot of last night's show has a direct bearing on her lesson?

a. If you do the first, it shows determination even when the odds are against you.

b. The second choice, dying of embarrassment, means you're willing to accept reality and deal with it — even when it's ugly.

c. If you choose to bluff, the teacher will realize you have a quick mind, at least. But she may wonder why you don't put it to better use!

More School Style!

Here's how I feel about school in general:_____

_____

_____

_____

_____

I do think school will be important to my future because:_____

_____

_____

_____

Speaking Out About Sports

Team sports are the best!

Strawberry

This is what I have to say about sports!

I like to play these sports:_____

_____

_____

I (circle one) like team sports / solo sports better

because:_____

_____

_____

This is my favorite sport to watch on TV:_____

_____because:_____

_____

_____

Draw or paste in a sports moment

And this is my favorite sport to watch during the

Olympics:_____

because:_____

_____

_____

After school, I participate in these sports:_____

_____

_____

In gym class, my favorite activity is:_____

_____because:_____

_____

_____

_____

I've played on these teams:_____

_____

_____

_____

My proudest moment as an athlete was definitely:_____

_____

_____

_____

_____

I like this sport_____,but

I'd like to become better at it because:_____

_____

_____

_____

And if I could make up a sport of my own, these would

be some of its rules:_____

_____

_____

_____

_____

What's your favorite place on a team?

Your Team Position

What does it say about your personality?

If it's OFFENSE, you always state your own opinion — even if others don't want to hear it.

If it's DEFENSE, you like to watch for a while before you jump into a new situation.

If it's GOALIE, you like to protect the people who are important to you.

If it's PITCHER, you like to be in the middle of everything and get your hands dirty.

If it's OUTFIELD, your thoughts tend to go a mile a minute — sometimes you find it hard to concentrate.

If it's on the BENCH, you're always supportive of your friends.

Test your
fitness factor
— active girls rule!

Fast Track

A Quiz

Answer each question
below, then add up
your score and read on
to find out how active
you are — and what
it might mean.

Cherry

1. A bunch of kids are playing softball. You:

   a. ask to be the pitcher
   b. get a great seat on the bleachers
   c. hope you're picked for right field

2. During gym you:

   a. keep up with everyone else
   b. keep moving to the back of the line
   c. volunteer to be team captain

3. When swimming you:

   a. mostly float
   b. mix the crawl with the sidestroke
      and breaststroke
   c. only do the crawl stroke

4. On a nice spring afternoon you think
   it would be fun to:

   a. read in a hammock
   b. organize a game of touch football
   c. play badminton with a friend

5. When running a race you:

    a. run to win
    b. do your best
    c. take care not to strain yourself

Add Up Your Score

Give yourself the following points for each answer:

1.	a = 5	b = 3	c = 1
2.	a = 3	b = 1	c = 5
3.	a = 1	b = 5	c = 3
4.	a = 1	b = 5	c = 3
5.	a = 5	b = 3	c = 1

Here's What Your Score Means

Fast Mover!   17 to 25 points
You're a fast mover who plays to win. You love the action and the competition involved in any sport.

Active!   10 to 16 points
You're active, but not athletic — you'd rather shoot hoops than play a whole basketball game. You like to move but you couldn't care less about counting up your points!

Mind Matters!   5 to 9 points
Sports just aren't your thing — you'd rather read or go to the movies. To you, the mind matters more than the body.

Conclusion

You probably know a lot more about yourself than you did when you opened this book. And you probably had fun along the way!

You can come back to these questions again and again, since your answers will be different as you change and grow.

Even before that, though, you can show the world what you're all about.

You're strong. You're special. You're a girl — and you're loving every minute of it!